EXPLORING WORLD CULTURES

Zimbabwe

Alicia Z. Klepeis

Cavendish Square
New York

Published in 2018 by Cavendish Square Publishing, LLC
243 5th Avenue, Suite 136, New York, NY 10016

Copyright © 2018 by Cavendish Square Publishing, LLC

First Edition

Library of Congress Cataloging-in-Publication Data

Names: Klepeis, Alicia, 1971- author.
Title: Zimbabwe / Alicia Z. Klepeis.
Other titles: Exploring world cultures.
Description: New York : Cavendish Square Publishing, 2018. |
Series: Exploring world cultures
Identifiers: LCCN 2016046391 (print) | LCCN 2016046743 (ebook) |
ISBN 9781502624963 (pbk.) | ISBN 9781502624970 (6 pack) |
ISBN 9781502624987 (library bound) | ISBN 9781502624994 (E-book)
Subjects: LCSH: Zimbabwe--Juvenile literature. | Zimbabwe--Civilization.
Classification: LCC DT2889 .K54 2017 (print) | LCC DT2889 (ebook) |
DDC 968.91--dc23
LC record available at "https://lccn.loc.gov/2016046391"

Editorial Director: David McNamara
Editor: Kristen Susienka
Copy Editor: Rebecca Rohan
Associate Art Director: Amy Greenan
Designer: Joseph Macri
Production Coordinator: Karol Szymczuk
Photo Research: J8 Media

Printed in the United States of America

Contents

Introduction 4

Chapter 1   Geography   6

Chapter 2   History   8

Chapter 3   Government   10

Chapter 4   The Economy   12

Chapter 5   The Environment   14

Chapter 6   The People Today   16

Chapter 7   Lifestyle   18

Chapter 8   Religion   20

Chapter 9   Language   22

Chapter 10   Arts and Festivals   24

Chapter 11   Fun and Play   26

Chapter 12   Food   28

Glossary 30

Find Out More 31

Index and About the Author 32

Introduction

Zimbabwe is a country in Africa. It has many special traditions and celebrations. People have lived in Zimbabwe for thousands of years. Different groups ruled what is now Zimbabwe during its history. Zimbabwe is a free country today.

Many people in Zimbabwe work on farms. They grow food and raise animals. But Zimbabweans have other kinds of jobs too. Some work in hospitals or schools. Others work in mines or factories. People in Zimbabwe also work in shops, hotels, and national parks.

There are many beautiful places to visit in Zimbabwe. The country has waterfalls, mountains, grasslands, and valleys. Visitors come from all over the world to see Zimbabwe's wildlife and historical sites.

Zimbabweans enjoy music, the **arts**, and books. People also like playing sports here.

Zimbabwe is a fascinating country to explore.

Two lions charge through the grasslands of Zimbabwe.

Zimbabwe is part of Africa. It is a little bigger than the state of Montana and covers 150,872 square miles (390,757 square kilometers).

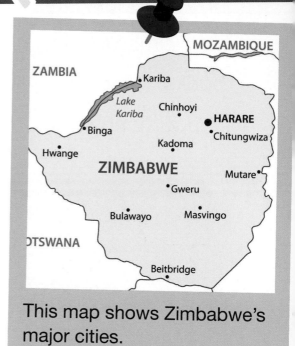

This map shows Zimbabwe's major cities.

Zimbabwe borders Botswana, Mozambique, South Africa, and Zambia. It is surrounded by land. It has several important rivers, like the Zambezi, Limpopo, Lundi, and Sabi Rivers. Lake Kariba borders Zimbabwe to the northwest.

Most of Zimbabwe is a high **plateau**. A ridge-like area called the Highveld runs from the country's southwest to its northeast. Elevations in the Highveld are usually 4,000 feet (1,219 meters) or more above sea level. This area is excellent for farming. Zimbabwe also has mountains.

Zimbabwe's climate is not too hot and not too cold.

Zimbabwe's Animals and Plants

Zimbabwe has many interesting plants, such as mopane and baobab trees. It is also home to baboons, martial eagles, and elephants.

A female chacma baboon rests atop a tree.

People have lived in Zimbabwe for thousands of years. This land was not always called Zimbabwe, though. It has also been called Rhodesia, Southern Rhodesia, and Zimbabwe Rhodesia.

The Great Enclosure, built from blocks of cut granite, is part of Great Zimbabwe.

By around the fifth century CE, **Bantu** peoples arrived here. A group called the Shona people started building a stone structure called Great Zimbabwe around 1250 CE. Great Zimbabwe was an important trading and religious center.

Things changed when Europeans arrived in the 1800s. In 1889, Britain sent settlers to Southern Rhodesia. It wasn't until 1980 that Zimbabwe became an independent country with the name it has today.

FACT!

The bird on Zimbabwe's flag is based on a carving found in the ruins at Great Zimbabwe, which date back to the eleventh century.

Zimbabwe has had many problems since its independence. Problems include **corruption**, unemployment, and not enough food. Zimbabweans hope their future will be better.

Robert Mugabe

Robert Mugabe was Zimbabwe's first prime minister. He has been in office since 1980.

Zimbabwe's government has three parts:

Zimbabwean presidential guards ride past the parliament building.

1) Legislative: This part of the government is known as Parliament. People in Parliament write new laws.

2) Judicial: The courts make up this part of Zimbabwe's government. They follow the country's constitution. It describes all of Zimbabwe's basic laws.

FACT!

Citizens of Zimbabwe can vote when they are eighteen years old.

3) Executive: The president, vice presidents (Zimbabwe has two), and the **cabinet** ministers make up this part of the government. The president is the head of state and runs the government.

Zimbabwe's parliament is made up of two groups. The Senate has 80 members. The National Assembly has 270 members. Parliament meets to pass laws in Harare, the country's capital.

Women in Government

Over 47 percent of Zimbabwean senators are female.

The Economy

Zimbabwe has a growing **economy**. Under its soil lie minerals like gold, nickel, copper, and coal. Mining earns lots of money for the country. Zimbabwe trades with countries all over the world. South Africa and

A gold miner works in Independence Mine.

China are two of its most important trading partners.

FACT!

Zimbabwe has a large supply of chromium. This element is used in steelmaking.

Two out of three Zimbabweans work in agriculture. Farmers in Zimbabwe grow many crops like corn, cotton, and coffee. Farmers here also raise animals like sheep, pigs, and goats. About one-quarter of people in Zimbabwe have service jobs.

Zimbabwe's 100-million-dollar note.

Some work as teachers or doctors. Others are shopkeepers, bankers, or hotel workers.

Factories in Zimbabwe make many products. Examples include steel, cement, and clothing.

Zimbabwe's Money

For many years, the country's money was the Zimbabwean dollar. In 2009, people in Zimbabwe started using US dollars and South African rand for money.

The Environment

Zimbabwe's animals, plants, and people need clean water and air to live. Some places in Zimbabwe do not have these things. Automobile traffic is one cause of **pollution**. Burning trash, such as car tires and plastic products, is another.

Harare's central business district has a lot of smoke and pollution.

Zimbabwean Wildlife

Hippos, rhinoceroses, and elephants are just a few of Zimbabwe's amazing animals. The government tries to protect them in national parks and wildlife reserves.

Many of Zimbabwe's rivers and dams are also polluted. Bad air from cars and chemicals put in the water make the water unclean. Chemicals can make people very sick.

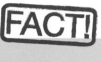

More than 36 percent of Zimbabwe's electricity comes from waterpower.

The Kariba Dam helps generate electicity.

Sometimes Zimbabwe has droughts. This makes it difficult to farm. People have cut many trees for cooking food, building houses, and other businesses. This hurts the animals that live there.

The People Today

Over fourteen million people live in Zimbabwe. Most people live in the countryside. Others have moved to cities and towns. Most of Zimbabwe's leaders belong to the Shona group. The Shona is the largest group of people in Zimbabwe.

A traditional Shona healer stands in front of a hut in his village.

The San

The San are considered southern Africa's first people. A small number of them live in Zimbabwe today.

The second-largest group is the Ndebele. Today many Ndebele live in southwestern Zimbabwe. During Zimbabwe's history, there has been conflict between the Shona and the Ndebele.

FACT!

Zimbabwe's biggest city, Harare, is home to over 1.5 million people. It is also the capital.

Zimbabwe is home to a number of smaller groups. These include the Batonga, Venda, and Shangaan peoples. All of these groups have their own special traditions.

People in Zimbabwe live in different ways. About two out of three Zimbabweans live in the countryside. People raise animals and grow food to sell or for their families to eat.

A young woman carries a bundle of firewood on her head.

The pace of life is often slower in the countryside. Women and girls here usually do the household work. They often have to gather firewood for cooking. They carry water long distances. Boys

FACT!

More than 72 percent of Zimbabweans live in poverty.

and men take care of the livestock, such as cattle.

About one-third of Zimbabwe's people live in cities and towns. The roles of men and women have changed more in the cities.

Skyscrapers in Zimbabwe's capital city, Harare.

Women may work in the government, schools, or other businesses.

Divided Families

Sometimes there isn't enough work in the countryside to support a family. Some Zimbabwean men take work in the cities and leave their families back home on the family farm.

Religion

Zimbabwe has no official religion. All Zimbabweans can believe in what they want. However, religion is important to many Zimbabwean people.

The majority of people are Christian. Many Zimbabwean

People worship in many different ways in Zimbabwe.

Christians are Protestant or Roman Catholic. They share some traditions and beliefs. They celebrate Easter and Christmas. Some go to church every week, while others do not.

In the countryside, many people practice traditional religions. The Shona people believe in

The city of Harare is home to places of worship for many faiths.

a god called Mwari. The Ndebele god is uMlimu. Zimbabweans often believe in the spirits of their ancestors who have died. Some people are said to communicate with these spirits.

About half of Zimbabwe's people practice a mixture of different beliefs. For example, a person might follow some Christian practices but also celebrate traditional religious ideas.

Spiritual Healers

Some people seek the help of a *nganga*, or spiritual healer, to treat their health problems.

A traffic sign in Harare's financial district points the way to the city's international airport.

People in Zimbabwe speak many languages. Shona, Ndebele, sign language, and English are four of Zimbabwe's sixteen official languages. Shona is the most widely spoken language. Ndebele is the second most commonly spoken

FACT!

Zimbabwe comes from two words in the Shona language: *dzimba,* meaning "houses," and *mabwe,* meaning "stones."

language. Many people in Zimbabwe speak more than one language.

Zimbabwe's government uses English. It is also the language used in business and law. Lots of Zimbabwean authors also write in English.

Learn a Little Ndebele

If you want to say "Hello," say, "*Sawubona.*" "How are you?" is "*Linjani?*"

People in Zimbabwe create many kinds of art. Music is an important part of their culture. Much of Zimbabwe's music is influenced by traditional sounds and rhythms. Local instruments include the

This is the correct way to hold (and play) a mbira.

mbira and the marimba. The mbira is sometimes called a "thumb piano." The marimba is a kind of xylophone made of wood.

Zimbabwe is known for its sculptures. Many are made of local stone, such as serpentine and verdite.

There are festivals throughout the year in Zimbabwe. Some are religious celebrations like Easter. Others are connected to different ethnic groups. Zimbabwe also has several public holidays. People celebrate Independence Day on April 18. This holiday marks the day in 1980 when Zimbabwe became an independent nation. Zimbabweans celebrate with speeches, parades, and the release of white doves.

Tuku: Zimbabwean Musician

Oliver "Tuku" Mtukudzi is a Zimbabwean songwriter and musician. He often sings about the challenges of everyday life in his homeland.

There are lots of ways to have fun in Zimbabwe. Many Zimbabweans enjoy sports. The most popular sport here is soccer. The Zimbabwe Premier Soccer League has sixteen teams.

Player Brian Chari in action during a cricket match.

Cricket is another popular sport in Zimbabwe. It is similar to baseball and came from England. Zimbabweans play professional cricket at home and in international competitions like the World Cricket Cup.

Both Zimbabweans and tourists enjoy nature. The country has many national parks and wildlife preserves. People can camp, hike, and go on safaris.

Kristy Coventry

Swimmer Kristy Coventry has won seven Olympic medals for Zimbabwe. She won three at the 2004 Olympics in Athens and four at the 2008 Olympics in Beijing.

Many people in Zimbabwe enjoy playing games. *Tsoro* is a traditional board game there. It involves moving stones along the rows of holes in the board.

FACT!

Kids in Zimbabwe often make their own toys from wire and other scrap materials.

People in Zimbabwe eat many kinds of fruits and vegetables. Zimbabweans often eat yams, spinach, and pumpkins. Mangoes, papayas, and bananas are popular too.

Sadza is served with fresh greens.

There is not a huge variety in the diet of most Zimbabweans. Corn is served in some form at almost every meal. *Sadza* is a cornmeal porridge. It might be sweetened at breakfast but served with vegetables at lunch.

Sadza is inexpensive to make. It is also pretty nutritious. People also eat corn on the cob as a snack. Meat is only eaten occasionally, depending on what a family can afford. Peanuts are part of many Zimbabwean dishes.

Beer is a popular beverage for adults in Zimbabwe. *Mazoe* (mah-ZOH-ee) is a drink made from fruit.

Insects as Food

Rural Zimbabweans often eat insects as part of their diet. Mopane worms, crickets, and flying ants are some examples. They are full of protein and minerals.

Glossary

arts   Any type of entertainment that is appreciated by people. Most common examples are theater, music, and artwork.

Bantu   A group of African people in southern and central Africa. They have their own language.

cabinet   A group of advisors who help the political head of a government.

corruption Dishonest behavior by those in power.

economy   The activities of a country that bring the country money.

plateau   A flat area of high ground.

pollution   Chemicals and other harmful things that make air or water dirty.

Find Out More

Books

Pearce, Winifred. *African Fables: Tales from Rhodesia (now Zimbabwe)*. Irvine, CA: Stalbridge Press, 2015.

Trent, Tererai. *The Girl Who Buried Her Dreams In a Can*. New York: Viking Books for Young Readers, 2015.

Website

National Geographic: Zimbabwe Facts

http://travel.nationalgeographic.com/travel/countries/zimbabwe-facts

Video

Our Africa: Zimbabwe

http://www.our-africa.org/zimbabwe

This website offers videos such as interviews with kids about soccer, music, and daily life in Zimbabwe.

Index

animals, 4, 7, 13–15, 18

arts, 5

Bantu, 8

cabinet, 11

corruption, 9

economy, 12

farmers, 12–13

language, 22–23

plateau, 6

pollution, 14

About the Author

Alicia Z. Klepeis began her career at the National Geographic Society. She is the author of many kids' books, including *The World's Strangest Foods*, *Bizarre Things We've Called Medicine*, *Francisco's Kites*, and *A Time for Change*. She lives with her family in upstate New York.